Power Prayers & Proclamations

The Power of Speaking God's Word

Mimika Cooney

Mimika Media

Mimika Media

Contents

Foreward

I wrote this mini book as a handy reference for whenever you need to refresh your walk with God. We all sin, and just like taking a daily shower, these prayers are a spiritual shower. They are most effective when spoken aloud with confidence and conviction. Declare the Word of God out loud and watch God move in your life in miraculous ways!

INVITATION

As a thank you for purchasing this book I would love to gift you with the digital version of the accompanying Prayer Cards. Print them out as easy prayer prompts. Claim your special gift by visiting:

https://www.mimikacooney.com/powerprayers

PROCLAMATIONS

What does it mean to "proclaim"? We hear this word often in the bible, and underestimate its importance. According to Webster's Dictionary[1], the word "proclaim" means: "*to declare publicly, typically insistently, proudly, or defiantly and in either speech or writing, to give outward indication of, to declare or declare to be solemnly, officially, or formally, to praise or glorify openly or publicly*".

Using your mouth to speak words of power to proclaim your authority through Christ, is to wield the sword of truth in this battle against spiritual forces of evil. Child of God, get your sword out and open your mouth to proclaim, declare and decree what is rightfully yours!

---

1. Proclaim https://www.merriam-webster.com/dictionary/proclaim

Chapter 1

Accept Christ

Romans 10:9 NIV
If you declare with your mouth, "Jesus is
Lord," and believe in your heart that God
raised him from the dead, you will be saved.

Lord I believe that you are the Son of God who died on the cross and rose again. I am a sinner. Please forgive me of my sins. Wash me clean with the blood of Jesus. By faith, I receive the gift of salvation and eternal life. I ask you now to come live in my heart. I am ready to trust you as my Lord and Saviour. Amen!

CHAPTER 2

CONFESSION OF SINS

1 John 1:9 NIV
If we confess our sins, he is faithful and just
and will forgive us our sins and purify us
from all unrighteousness.

LORD I HUMBLY COME before you and ask for your forgiveness of all my sins. I repent of all known and unknown sins I've committed that have affected my calling, my destiny, my purpose, my health, my soul, my relationships and my walk with you. As an act of my will, and using the words of my mouth, I confess my sins and repent and turn from my wicked ways. I detach myself from any accusation, hold or agreement the enemy may have had over me through sin. By the authority of Jesus Christ I tear up the contracts that tie me to any and all demonic activity, authority and interference that has gained access to my life through my sins. I shut the doors and seal them shut with the blood of Jesus. Thank you Lord for redeeming me making me new and redeeming my bloodline in Jesus name! Tip: Take communion as a physical act of obedience and surrender.

Chapter 3

Forgiveness of Sins

Ephesians 1:7 NIV
In him we have redemption through his
blood, the forgiveness of sins, in accordance
with the riches of God's grace.

Lord thank you for dying on the cross to redeem me from my sins. Please forgive the sins I've committed (both knowingly and unknowingly) and I ask that you heal all the wounds in my soul. Please forgive the sins of my generational line and all past sins passed down through the generations through the third and fourth generation. I repent of all sin, transgressions and iniquity, and humble myself and my bloodline under your mighty hand. I believe you are washing me clean, healing me of all trauma, and cleansing all soul wounds in my bloodline. I believe you love me unconditionally and cause me to break through. I thank you and praise you in advance for victory, in Jesus name!

CHAPTER 4

ARMOUR OF GOD

Ephesians 6:10-12 NIV

[10] Finally, be strong in the Lord and in his mighty power. [11] Put on the full armour of God, so that you can take your stand against the devil's schemes. [12] For our struggle is not against flesh and blood, but against the rulers, against the authorities, against the powers of this dark world and against the spiritual forces of evil in the heavenly realms.

LORD THANK YOU FOR the helmet of salvation, breastplate of righteousness, belt of truth, shield of faith, sword of the spirit, and the readiness of gospel of peace on my feet. I wield my weapons of warfare to fight off the fiery darts of the devil. I ask for your divine protection in Jesus name amen! Tip: Pray this every single morning as you wake to protect you for the day.

CHAPTER 5

DELIVERANCE PRAYER

2 Chronicles 20:17 NIV
You will not have to fight this battle. Take up your positions; stand firm and see the deliverance the Lord will give you, Judah and Jerusalem. Do not be afraid; do not be discouraged. Go out to face them tomorrow, and the Lord will be with you.

LORD I BELIEVE YOU are the Son of God, that you died for my sins on the cross and rose again from the dead. I submit myself to You and accept you as my Lord and Saviour. I repent of all sins and rebellion and ask for your forgiveness. Release me from all curses from my own sin, and from the consequences of my ancestors sins of iniquity back to the third and fourth generation. Every sin past the fourth generation is sealed by the blood of Jesus and statute of limitations. By an act of my will I forgive and release all who have harmed me (both knowingly and unknowingly) just as God forgives me. I renounce all contact with the satanic and the occult and break its power and any claims Satan has against me. Show me if I have contact objects so I can commit to destroying them. I believe Jesus took on every curse on the cross so that I can live freely. Please release me now from every curse over my life in the mighty name of Jesus Christ!

CHAPTER 6

HUSBANDS AND WIVES

Ephesians 5:33 NIV
However, each one of you also must love his
wife as he loves himself, and the wife must
respect her husband.

LORD THANK YOU FOR giving me the gift of my spouse. I repent of the sin of rebellion and cancel the effects of the curse of rebellion. As an act of my will, I come under the authority of my spouse as head of our home, and under the authority of Jesus Christ. I pray Lord that you guide my spouse with divine wisdom, discernment and understanding. I thank you, God that you are knitting our souls together as one flesh through our marriage covenant. I declare that no weapon formed against us will prosper. I cast down all vain imaginations and attacks in Jesus name. I plead the blood of Jesus over my spouse, our marriage and our family. Thank you, Lord for breaking through spiritual barriers as we align as one, in Jesus name amen!

CHAPTER 7

HEALING PRAYER

Proverbs 16:24 NIV
Gracious words are a honeycomb, sweet to
the soul and healing to the bones.

LORD I DECLARE THAT you died for me and by faith I claim perfect health in Jesus name. I repent for opening the doors to the enemy. I resist the devil and break off his hold on me in Jesus name. Cleanse my blood with the powerful blood of Jesus. By the power and authority of the matchless name of Jesus Christ I take authority over every virus, bacteria and illness in my body. I purge every toxin and poison; I curse every pathogen and it must leave my body now in Jesus name. Strengthen my immune system as I declare by His stripes I am healed! I release health and restoration throughout my body by the dunamis resurrection power. I command all diseases, inflammation and swelling to go now in Jesus name. All pathogens, flu, viruses, parasites and demons that have caused diseases must come out now in Jesus name! Spirits of fear, death, sickness and infirmity I command you to leave me now in Jesus name! Restore my DNA and every cell in my body to perfect health, and reverse any destruction and degeneration. Realign my frequencies to God's divine design for my body, and make it strong to fight all attacks in Jesus name!

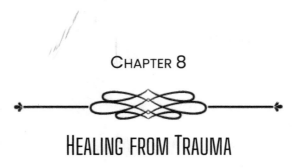

CHAPTER 8

HEALING FROM TRAUMA

Matthew 11:28-30 NIV
Come to me, all you who are weary and
burdened, and I will give you rest. Take my
yoke upon you and learn from me, for I am
gentle and humble in heart, and you will find
rest for your souls. For my yoke is easy and
my burden is light.

LORD THANK YOU FOR sending your Son Jesus to die on the cross for me. Thank you that the blood of Jesus cleanses me and sets me free. As an act of my will, I choose to release the pain of my past trauma. I ask for You to forgive my sin of unforgiveness, and for agreeing with the lies of the devil. I receive the gift of healing through Jesus's death and resurrection. All open doors from trauma that allowed the enemy to attack me are now sealed closed in Jesus name. I release the dunamis power of healing into all areas of my body and soul. Thank You for my complete healing in Jesus name amen!

CHAPTER 9

RELEASE HEALING

Malachi 4:2 NIV
But for you who revere my name, the sun
of righteousness will rise with healing in
its rays. And you will go out and frolic like
well-fed calves.

LORD I DECREE THE Son of Righteousness is arising on me now with healing in his wings. The light rays of Jesus Christ is filling me right now. I receive healing in my mind, will and emotions. Jesus is curing me in my physical body of all attacks in my eyes, my ears, my mind, my atom cells, my bones and any of my 12 systems. I receive healing in my Integumentary System, Skeletal System, Muscular System, Nervous System, Endocrine System, Cardiovascular System, Lymphatic System, Respiratory System, Digestive System, Urinary System, and Reproductive System. I am filled with the light of Christ because Jesus is arising on me with healing in his wings and his beams of light permeate every cell in my body, in Jesus name amen!

CHAPTER 10

Praying for Others

James 5:16 NIV
Therefore confess your sins to each other
and pray for each other so that you may be
healed. The prayer of a righteous person is
powerful and effective.

LORD I COME BEFORE you with a humble heart. I repent of all wrongdoing and turn from my wicked ways. I ask that you grant my petition to stand in the gap for NAME. You Lord know their situation better than I do and I ask that according to your Word in Mark 11:24 you say "I tell you, you can pray for anything, and if you believe that you've received it, it will be yours." I believe that Jesus you are the Son of God who died on the cross for our sins. I ask that you cover NAME with the blood of Jesus and you forgive them for they know not what they do. I ask that you forgive their sins of (list sins) and cleanse them of all unrighteousness. Please Lord soften their heart to receive the gospel and save them so that they come to salvation. I pray the angels to encamp around them and a hedge of protection be their shield. I thank you and praise you for all that you are doing in their lives to bring them into the Kingdom and deliver them from darkness and their afflictions in Jesus name amen!

CHAPTER 11

STANDING IN THE GAP

Ezekiel 22:30 NIV
I looked for someone among them who
would build up the wall and stand before
me in the gap on behalf of the land so I
would not have to destroy it, but I found no
one.

LORD I STAND IN your courts and repent on behalf of NAME. Please show him/her mercy and ask for your blood to speak for her/him. Lord save them by bringing them to salvation. I repent for any lie he/she has believed about her/himself and ask for forgiveness. I repent for all words I have spoken in frustration, anger or complaints made about NAME. I ask that the words held against NAME be dismissed and their power annulled. Let him/her go free and I ask this be recorded as evidence in your courts. I declare that NAME is ordained by you and I ask he/she will step into their divine purpose now. I rebuke the spirits of e.g. anxiety and declare you have no power against NAME, your rights are revoked. I thank you Lord for releasing NAME today in Jesus name amen!

POSITIVE DECLARATIONS

Speak Aloud

WIELD THE SWORD OF truth by speaking these confessions out loud.

Psalm 118:17
I will not die but live, and will proclaim what the LORD has done.

Habakkuk 3:19
The Sovereign LORD is my strength; he makes my feet like the feet of a deer, he enables me to tread on the heights.

Isaiah 12:2
Surely God is my salvation; I will trust and not be afraid. The LORD, the LORD himself, is my strength and my defense; he has become my salvation.

Psalm 28:7
The LORD is my strength and my shield; my heart trusts in him, and he helps me. My heart leaps for joy, and with my song I praise him.

Psalm 46:2
Therefore we will not fear, though the earth give way and the mountains fall into the heart of the sea,

Jeremiah 17:8

They will be like a tree planted by the water that sends out its roots by the stream. It does not fear when heat comes; its leaves are always green. It has no worries in a year of drought and never fails to bear fruit."

Deuteronomy 28:3

You will be blessed in the city and blessed in the country.

Psalm 118:26

Blessed is he who comes in the name of the LORD. From the house of the LORD we bless you.

Release Prayers

Matthew 12:44-45 NIV
[44] Then it says, 'I will return to the house
I left.' When it arrives, it finds the house
unoccupied, swept clean and put in order.
[45] Then it goes and takes with it seven other
spirits more wicked than itself, and they go
in and live there. And the final condition of
that person is worse than the first. That is
how it will be with this wicked generation."

Why is it important to speak words of release and infilling? The scripture above shows us that if we pray to clean up our house (our temple), we need to fill it with the Holy Spirit so that demonic spirits have no legal right to return. It's important to invite the Lord to break off any holds the enemy has over you, then pray to be covered with the blood of Jesus as protection, and then to infill our mind, body and soul with His liquid love!

RELEASE FROM ANGER

Ephesians 4:26 NIV
In your anger do not sin": Do not let the sun
go down while you are still angry.

LORD THANK YOU FOR your grace and mercy. I ask for forgiveness for my angry outbursts and for losing control. I repent of the harsh, hard, pressing and destructive words I have used in a fit of rage. Please cleanse me of all unrighteousness and seal up with the blood of Jesus any open doors I have opened to the enemy by sinning by getting angry. I break off the spirit of anger in me and in my bloodline in Jesus name. I cancel all effects and break any curses that have had power over me and my family. Thank you Lord that you are healing every area of my body, spirit and soul. I release the resurrection dunamis power in me in Jesus name. I ask for forgiveness from those that I have hurt or wronged during my angry outbursts. Jesus please reconcile our relationship through your Holy Spirit and bring us into right covenant and forgiveness in Jesus name amen!

CHAPTER 14

RELEASE FROM ANXIETY

1 Peter 5:7 NIV
Cast all your anxiety on him because he
cares for you.

LORD THANK YOU FOR your unfailing love. I choose to place my trust in You. Please deliver me from anxiety and break off the spirit of fear. With your strength I take captive every negative thought that tries to steal my joy. I renounce my agreement with anxiety and fear and break its hold over me now in Jesus name. I repent for agreeing with the lies of the enemy and for not trusting you. I thank you Lord for delivering me from the spirit of fear and anxiety. I release joy, peace and love in Jesus name amen!

RELEASE FROM BITTERNESS

Ephesians 4:31 NIV
Get rid of all bitterness, rage and anger,
brawling and slander, along with every form
of malice.

LORD THANK YOU FOR the redeeming power of Jesus' sacrifice on the cross. I ask for forgiveness for the words and thoughts of bitterness I have allowed in my heart. I repent of my sin of bitterness. Please wash me with the blood of Jesus and cleanse me of any disease in my bones, my blood and my body that is a result of bitterness. I cancel all negative and destructive words of bitterness I have spoken over myself and others. I close all doors to the enemy that were opened due to my sin of bitterness and seal my mind, body and soul with the blood of Jesus. I receive your healing now in Jesus name amen!

CHAPTER 16

RELEASE FROM COMPLAINING

John 6:43-44 NIV
⁴³ Stop grumbling among yourselves," Jesus answered. ⁴⁴ No one can come to me unless the Father who sent me draws them, and I will raise them up at the last day.

LORD I THANK YOU for Jesus and that I can keep my eyes fixed on you. I repent of complaining and grumbling, I am grateful for all my blessings. Any words of complaints that I have spoken over myself and others, I now cancel and rescind. I cancel all negative effects my complaints have caused, and revoke any judgements in the courts of heaven. Thank you Lord for loosing and releasing the answer to my prayers, and opening the heavens over my situation in Jesus name!

RELEASE FROM CURSES

Deuteronomy 28:15-68 NIV
However, if you do not obey the Lord your
God and do not carefully follow all his com-
mands and decrees I am giving you today,
all these curses will come on you and over-
take you.

LORD THANK YOU FOR redeeming me from death by the sacrifice of Jesus's death on the cross, and the dunamis
resurrection power that lives in me. I repent for opening
the doors to curses in my life. I break and cancel every
effect from the curses of treachery, apostasy, disobedience, works of the flesh, and trusting in man. I cancel
every word curse I have spoken over myself and others.
I break all generational curses in my bloodline right back
to the third and fourth generation. All sins before the
fourth generation are no longer valid, and are sealed by
the statute of limitations. I revoke the claims the devil
has used against me and my family, and present the
blood of Jesus as evidence of my innocence. All sins and
accusations used by me are no longer valid. I cancel and
break all unscriptural covenants, all effects of witchcraft,
divination, fortune telling and all occult involvement by
my own actions and those of my bloodline. I repent of
idolatry and break curses brought on by making an idol

Connect with me Online

Website
https://www.mimikacooney.com
YouTube
https://youtube.com/c/mimikacooney
LinkedIn
https://www.linkedin.com/in/mimikacooney
Facebook
https://www.facebook.com/themimikacooney
Instagram
https://www.instagram.com/mimikacooney
Twitter
https://twitter.com/mimikacooney
Pinterest
https://www.pinterest.com/mimikacooney
Rumble
https://rumble.com/c/MimikaTV

More Books

If you enjoyed this book, check out other books in my collection:
www.mimikacooney.com/books

Worrier to Warrior
www.mimikacooney.com/warrior
Unstick Your Mind
www.mimikacooney.com/unstick
Mindset Make Over
www.mimikacooney.com/mindset

Share

If you enjoyed this book and found the content useful, please share it with your friends. Please tag me @mimikacooney and use the hashtag #PowerPrayers so I can thank you.

Join our Book Launch Team

https://mimikacooney.com/launchteam/

Extra Offers

Complimentary Study Guide

Download the free cards by going to:
  www.mimikacooney.com/powerprayers

Review

As an author, it is important to get **Reviews** from valuable readers like you, so that future readers can make better decisions. Your opinion is important and I truly value your feedback. Please help me by leaving your honest review on your preferred bookstore thank you!

More Free Resources

For a list of my other resources visit my website
  https://www.mimikacooney.com

Chapter 26

Release from Perfectionism

Ephesians 2:8-9 NIV
For it is by grace you have been saved,
through faith—and this is not from your-
selves, it is the gift of God— not by works,
so that no one can boast.

Lord thank you for the redeeming power of your son Jesus and that His death and resurrection that makes me
perfect in your eyes. I repent for allowing the negative
spirit of perfectionism to run my thoughts, words, and
actions. I ask for you to search my heart God and clear
out all destructive patterns, habits and mindsets. Make
my heart new and perfect toward You. I choose to do
Your will in my life and come into obedience under your
Word. Thank you for healing me in Jesus name amen!

CHAPTER 27

RELEASE FROM PRIDE

Proverbs 16:18 NIV
Pride goes before destruction, a haughty
spirit before a fall.

LORD PLEASE FORGIVE ME for allowing pride in my life. As I choose humility over pride, I humble myself before you. I confess that I have insisted on having my own way and clinging to pride. I ask for your forgiveness. Thank you for revealing to me where the roots of pride so that I can make amends. With the situation of CONFLICT that you have brought to my mind. Where pride has been a barrier, as an act of my will, I yield myself to you and release the pride that has held me captive. I choose to step away from pride. I humble myself and ask for their forgiveness. God I need your help and grace. I break off the spirit of pride and break its hold on me in Jesus' name. Please Lord give me eyes to see where pride has blinded me. I close every demonic door that pride has given access to in my life, and seal them shut with the blood of Jesus. Thank you God for your unconditional love and for my healing, in Jesus name amen! Tip: A good exercise is to go to the individuals you have hurt or argued with and ask for forgiveness as a step toward humbling yourself and activating your healing.

CHAPTER 28

RELEASE FROM NEGATIVE THOUGHTS

2 Corinthians 10:5 NIV
We demolish arguments and every preten-
sion that sets itself up against the knowl-
edge of God, and we take captive every
thought to make it obedient to Christ.

LORD I THANK YOU for the redeeming power of Jesus who died and was raised from the dead. I repent for dwelling on any negative, evil, wrong thought and bring my mind into obedience to Christ. I seal up any access points that my thoughts have given to the enemy. I seal my mind with the blood of Jesus and wear the helmet of salvation. I have the mind of Christ! Thank you for saving me in Jesus name amen!

CHAPTER 29

RELEASE FROM NEGATIVE WORDS

Proverbs 18:21 NIV
The tongue has the power of life and death,
and those who love it will eat its fruit.

LORD PLEASE FORGIVE THE negative and destructive words I have spoken against myself and others. I cancel all curses and negative consequences that have resulted from my negative speech. Please forgive me for agreeing with the enemy and speaking words of death and destruction. Any accusations I have made against others in the courts of heaven I now cancel and revoke in Jesus name. I declare I am made in the image of God. I have the mind of Christ and by Jesus stripes, I am healed. I claim my inheritance of love, joy and peace in the Holy Spirit, in Jesus name amen!

CHAPTER 30

RELEASE FROM OFFENSE

Proverbs 19:11 NIV
A person's wisdom yields patience; it is to
one's glory to overlook an offense.

LORD PLEASE FORGIVE ME for any sin with what I have said, knowingly or unknowingly, and reveal to me where I have erred so that I can repair what I broke and ask for forgiveness. Please forgive me for every offense I have had against anyone, both living and dead. Please help me to release them in love. Lord, I forgive NAME/S for offending me and ask that you forgive me for holding grudges in my heart. I retract my case in the courts of heaven accusing them of offense towards me. I accept the fact that I have been hurt, but I will not allow that to stick to my spirit and my heart. I release NAME/S now in Jesus name. Lord, detach me from any feelings of animosity and resentment. It will it to be removed from my life permanently. Heal my heart from any hurts. Seal up any holes that have opened up and close any ways that Satan has access to. Fill me with your love Lord Jesus, from the tip of my head to the soles of my toes. Your perfect love casts out all fear. Thank you for your forgiveness of my sins and redeeming me through Jesus blood sacrifice, in Jesus name amen!

RELEASE FROM REBELLION

1 Samuel 15:23 NIV
For rebellion is like the sin of divination, and arrogance like the evil of idolatry. Because you have rejected the word of the Lord, he has rejected you as king."

LORD THANK YOU FOR Jesus and the work of the Cross. I declare that I have received life because Jesus was willing to die for me. I repent of all my sins of rebellion and witchcraft against my authority figures NAME/S. I now come to obedience in Christ Jesus. I break off, bind and cancel the curses in my generational line that are because of disobedience, rebellion and witchcraft from the acts of my ancestors (right back to the third and fourth generation). By an act of my will and words of my mouth, I humbly come under your authority in all areas of my life. I receive your forgiveness of sins, grace and mercy for me and my family in Jesus name amen!

RELEASE FROM REJECTION

1 Peter 2:4 NIV
As you come to him, the living Stone—rejected by humans but chosen by God and precious to him.

LORD THANK YOU FOR sending your Son to die for me and for taking on rejection so that I don't have be rejected. I ask for your forgiveness for harbouring bitterness, resentment, rebellion and hatred in my heart toward NAME/S. I break off all traces of the root of rejection from my mind, heart, body and soul. I repent for agreeing with the enemy and cancel all negative words I've spoken over myself. I break agreement with the spirit of rejection over my life and my past and future generational line. I detach myself and my identity from being rejected as my identity is in you alone Jesus. I receive your love and acceptance through Christ Jesus. I declare and decree I am a child of God who is loved and accepted unconditionally, in Jesus name amen!

CHAPTER 33

RELEASE FROM RELIGIOUS SPIRIT

James 1:26 NIV
Those who consider themselves religious
and yet do not keep a tight rein on their
tongues deceive themselves, and their religion is worthless.

LORD THANK YOU FOR the redeeming power of the cross. I repent of judging and criticizing others according to a set of man-made rules. I break off the spirit of religion from myself and my generational line. I cancel all curses of disobedience and pride due to the spirit of religion. Please forgive me and my generational line for opening the door to the blindness of the spirit of religion. I break its power of me and detach myself from all legal areas it has gained in my life. I seal my mind and heart with the blood of Jesus. Thank you God that you are lifting the veil off my eyes and my loved ones so that your message of grace is revealed to our hearts in Jesus name amen!

CHAPTER 34

RELEASE FROM RESENTMENT

Job 5:2 NIV
Resentment kills a fool, and envy slays the
simple.

LORD PLEASE FORGIVE ME for agreeing with the spirit of resentment, and for allowing it access to my life. I repent for
holding resentment, hatred and unforgiveness toward
NAME/S. Lord remove the sting of resentment and its
roots from my heart so that it no longer has any power
over my mind, my will or my emotions. I detach myself
from any agreement I have might (both knowingly and
unknowingly) with resentment and cancel its power now
in Jesus' name amen!

CHAPTER 35

RELEASE FROM SELF PITY

Psalm 69:20 NIV
Scorn has broken my heart and has left me
helpless; I looked for sympathy, but there
was none, for comforters, but I found none.

LORD THANK YOU GOD that your Word says you are my shepherd who guides me, so I never need to feel alone. Thank you that I lack nothing and for your comfort during dark days. Thank you for making me calm and refreshing my soul. Thank you for protecting me from the enemy. Please, Lord forgive me of my sins of selfishness. As an act of my will, I choose to focus on you and not my circumstances. I reject all forms of self-pity. Thank you for delivering me in Jesus name amen!

CHAPTER 36

RELEASE FROM SOUL TIES

1 Corinthians 6:16
Do you not know that he who unites himself with a prostitute is one with her in
body? For it is said, "The two will become
one flesh".

LORD I REPENT OF all ungodly soul ties, spiritual connections and emotional relationship I made with others (both knowingly and unknowingly), through illicit sex, fornication, blood agreements and verbal soul ties. I renounce and break all their power over me now in Jesus name. I receive your healing oil of anointing to cover all areas of my mind, body and soul, in Jesus name amen!

CHAPTER 37

RELEASE FROM SPIRITUAL ATTACKS

2 Corinthians 10:4 NIV
The weapons we fight with are not the
weapons of the world. On the contrary, they
have divine power to demolish strongholds.

LORD THANK YOU FOR the power of the name of Jesus and the word of my testimony. I repent for all sin and transgressions in my soul, that have allowed the enemy legal ground in my life. I cancel the plans and attacks of the enemy and send them back to hell never to return again. I seal my mind, body and soul with the blood of Jesus. I pray the angels to encamp around me and my family as a fortress of protection. Where I have opened any doors to the enemy and given him legal ground to attack me, I repent now and seal every door with the blood of Jesus. Thank you for the Holy Spirit fire of protection that guards my heart and mind, in Jesus name amen!

CHAPTER 38

RELEASE FROM STRESS

Philippians 4:6-7 NIV
[6] Do not be anxious about anything, but in every situation, by prayer and petition, with thanksgiving, present your requests to God. [7] And the peace of God, which transcends all understanding, will guard your hearts and your minds in Christ Jesus.

LORD THANK YOU GOD for caring so much for me that you want me to be well. I repent for allowing stress to affect my mind, body and soul. Please forgive my acts of disobedience and for not listening to your warnings of when to stop and slow down. I detach myself from the ill effects of toxic stress on every cell in my body. I release the joy of the Lord as my strength. I receive healing in all my cells down to the atom level. Renew my mitochondria energy cells and revive all damaged and destroyed areas of my body. I release the dunamis healing power to flood every cell in my body and repair all damage in Jesus name!

CHAPTER 39

RELEASE FROM UNFORGIVENESS

Matthew 6:14-15 NIV
¹⁴ For if you forgive other people when they sin against you, your heavenly Father will also forgive you. ¹⁵ But if you do not forgive others their sins, your Father will not forgive your sins.

LORD I FORGIVE NAME/S for SINS just as I want You to forgive me. Thank you for your forgiveness and for redeeming me from my sins of unforgiveness. As an act of my will, I release NAME/S in forgiveness and pray your blessings over them/him/her. I detach myself from all curses and blockages that unforgiveness has given access to in my life. I declare the dunamis power is released into every area of my soul and body and is healing me right now. Please Lord release any blockages, holds, barriers and barricades that have hindered me from walking in your will for my life. Open my eyes and ears to hear you clearly. Thank You in Jesus name amen!

CHAPTER 40

RELEASE FROM WORRY

Proverbs 3:5-6 NIV
[5] Trust in the Lord with all your heart and lean not on your own understanding; [6] in all your ways submit to him, and he will make your paths straight.

LORD THANK YOU THAT your Word says that you don't give me a spirit of fear but divine power, love and a sound mind through Jesus. I thank you Lord that I can put my trust in You to work all things out for my good. I cast out the spirit of fear and worry and command it to go now in Jesus name. I plead the blood of Jesus over my mind and heart and protect myself with the armour of God so that I can fight off the attacks of the enemy. Thank you for delivering me in Jesus name amen!

Presented to

From

CHAPTER 25

RELEASE FROM JUDGEMENT

Romans 2:1 NIV
You, therefore, have no excuse, you who
pass judgment on someone else, for at
whatever point you judge another, you
are condemning yourself, because you who
pass judgment do the same things.

LORD THANK YOU FOR Your mercy and kindness. I ask for forgiveness for the words I've said and thoughts I've had in judgment and criticism towards NAME/S. Please forgive me for acting as judge and jury where I have no authority to judge. I repent of my sins, please release me from bondage. I release NAME/S in love and ask for you to release blessings into their life in Jesus' name amen!

out of anyone or anything other than God. I repent from bringing into my home any items that are an abomination and detestable to you Lord, and I break every curse associated with these items. I cancel and break all soul ties to other people, created through sexual immorality, word and blood covenants. I break all curses created through sexual immoral acts of fornication, adultery, perversion, and pornography. I repent of the act of abortion and murder and cancel the curse of death over myself and my bloodline. I repent for my words and actions of anti-semitism and break the effects of the curse. I repent for robbing You God from tithes and cancel the curse of poverty over my finances. I repent for believing and speaking false doctrine and cancel its effects. I repent for my acts of theft and stealing from the innocent. I repent for acts of perjury and speaking lies. I cancel, break and bind every curse in my life, in the lives of my immediate family and all future generations in my bloodline. Thank you Jesus for saving me and redeeming my life. I claim Gods blessings and abundance as my inheritance as a child of God in Jesus name! Tip: Take communion as a physical act of obedience and surrender.

CHAPTER 18

RELEASE FROM DEPRESSION

Psalm 143:7-8 NIV
Answer me quickly, Lord; my spirit fails. Do not hide your face from me or I will be like those who go down to the pit. Let the morning bring me word of your unfailing love, for I have put my trust in you. Show me the way I should go, for to you I entrust my life.

LORD THANK YOU FOR dying for me and for Your victory on the cross. I declare I am released from the torment of depression and oppression. My spirit, body, and soul are willing vessels of righteousness, completely surrendered to God for His service and His glory. I cancel any word agreements I have made, aligning myself and my identity with the spirit of depression. I break the power of depression over my mind, my will, my emotions, and my physical body. Make me a clean and living sacrifice for your glory Lord, in Jesus name amen!

CHAPTER 19

RELEASE FROM DECEPTION

1 John 4:3 NIV
But every spirit that does not acknowledge
Jesus is not from God. This is the spirit of the
antichrist, which you have heard is coming
and even now is already in the world.

LORD THANK YOU FOR bringing the truth of your Word into my life, because You love me. Please give me eyes to see, and ears to hear, so that I may embrace what I am learning. I thank you for the truth penetrating my mind and heart so that I may not be afraid of being led astray. Lord, I humbly ask for a radical increase in my love and desire for Your Word. I proclaim Your Word is the absolute truth that will protect me from deception. Please help me to never choose anything or anyone but You God. I break all agreements I have made (both knowingly or unknowingly) with the spirit of the antichrist of this age. I thank you for this freedom in Jesus amen!

CHAPTER 20

RELEASE FROM EXCESSIVE REASONING

1 Corinthians 1:27 NIV
But God chose the foolish things of the
world to shame the wise; God chose the
weak things of the world to shame the
strong.

LORD THANK YOU FOR giving me the Holy Spirit as my comforter and friend. I repent of excessive reasoning, of relying on my own strength and abilities, and for disobeying your instructions. Please forgive my lack of faith. I declare I set my mind on the will of God and I trust You to work all things out for my good. Lord please remove all mental blockages that are hindering me from hearing your voice clearly. Thank you for delivering me in Jesus name amen!

CHAPTER 21

RELEASE FROM FALSE IDENTITY

Ephesians 2:10 NIV
For we are God's handiwork, created in
Christ Jesus to do good works, which God
prepared in advance for us to do.

LORD I RENOUNCE MY agreement with the false identity that says I am not good enough, and which does not come into alignment with God's plan for my life. I detach myself from every word curse spoken over me, by me or by others, that has placed a demonic hold on my God-given identity and purpose. I break the power of perversion of every kind, confusion, lies, mixture, false belonging, false doctrine, false religion, false hope, and all lies masquerading as truth in my mind and generational line. I repent for believing the enemy's lies and agreeing with the false truths in my mind and heart. I repent for believing the words spoken over me by others that do not align with my true identity. Every spirit attached to me that has shifted my identity must leave now in Jesus name! I detach myself from the false identity that has perverted my true calling, purpose and identity. Thank you, God for knitting me together and for regenerating all damaged areas of my life. I declare that I am a new creature in Christ Jesus, and all things are made new in Jesus name!

CHAPTER 22

RELEASE FROM FEAR

1 John 4:18
There is no fear in love. But perfect love
drives out fear, because fear has to do with
punishment. The one who fears is not made
perfect in love.

LORD THANK YOU LORD for your promise to deliver me when
I call on your name. Please deliver me from the spirit of
fear and break off any hold it has on me. I forgive every
person who has hurt me and I release them in love. I
detach myself from every word curse and agreement I
made with fear. I repent for opening the doors to fear
through my eye gates and my ears from unclean things
I've seen and heard. I detach the spirit of fear now from
my mind, my heart, my body and my spirit. Release the
dunamis power into every crevice of my broken soul and
heal up the wounds of my past. I break and bind you spirit
of fear be gone now in Jesus name amen!

CHAPTER 23

RELEASE FROM GUILT, SHAME & CONDEMNATION

Isaiah 61:7
Instead of your shame you will receive a
double portion, and instead of disgrace you
will rejoice in your inheritance. And so you
will inherit a double portion in your land,
and everlasting joy will be yours.

LORD THANK YOU THAT your Word says there is no condemnation for those who are in Christ Jesus. As a child of God I claim my inheritance of love, joy and peace for I have the mind of Christ. I forgive those who have sinned and hurt me. I command the spirit of fear, guilt, shame and condemnation to leave me now in Jesus name. Thank you for the gift of freedom in Jesus. I receive your grace Lord and healing in my body and soul in Jesus name amen!

CHAPTER 24

RELEASE FROM JEALOUSY

Proverbs 27:4 NIV
Anger is cruel and fury overwhelming, but
who can stand before jealousy?

LORD I THANK YOU for the sacrifice Jesus made for me to be free. I repent of the sin of jealousy. I am grateful for all my blessings and put my trust in you God, to pour the blessings into my life that you have planned for me. I repent of the negative words I've spoken over others in my jealous state, and cancel their ill effects in Jesus name. I repent for allowing the spirit of jealousy to fester in my heart and mind. I trust you God to give me what I need, when I need it, in your timing and by Your will. I detach myself from the effects and consequences of jealousy, and loose the spirit of joy and thanksgiving in my life in Jesus name amen!